JESUS
THE ONE
AND ONLY
LEADER GUIDE

Beth Moore

LifeWay Press®
Nashville, Tennessee

ITEM 001116515
ISBN 0-7673-3276-8

This book is the text for course CG-0525
in the subject area Personal Life in the Christian Growth Study Plan.

Dewey Decimal Classification: 232.901
Subject heading: BIBLE-STUDY AND TEACHING; JESUS CHRIST-BIOGRAPHY

To order additional copies of this resource:
Write to LifeWay Church Resources Customer Service; One LifeWay Plaza; Nashville, TN 37234-0113;
fax (615) 251-5933; phone (800) 458-2772; e-mail *orderentry@lifeway.com* order online at *www.lifeway.com;*
or visit the LifeWay Christian Store serving you.

Printed in the United States of America

Leadership and Adult Publishing
LifeWay Church Resources
One LifeWay Plaza
Nashville, TN 37234-0175

Introduction

Jesus the One and Only is an in-depth study of the life of Christ based on the Book of Luke. The goal of our study is to get to know Jesus intimately—as though we had walked with Him during His days of earthly ministry.

This guide has been prepared to equip you to plan and lead a study of *Jesus the One and Only* for groups in your church or community. You will find administrative guidance, help for planning and promoting the study, and step-by-step instructions for conducting the group-study sessions.

COURSE OVERVIEW

This in-depth course was designed to be completed over 11 weeks through a combination of daily, individual study, and weekly group sessions.

Individual study. Each participant needs a copy of the *Jesus the One and Only* member book, which contains reading assignments and activities designed to reinforce and apply learning. The member book is divided into an introduction and 10 weeks of content. Every week's material contains 5 daily lessons, each requiring about 45 minutes to complete. Participants complete the daily reading and the learning activities at home in preparation for the weekly group sessions.

Group sessions. Participants meet once each week for a two-hour group session that guides them to discuss and apply what they have learned during their daily, individual study. The small-group portion of this session encourages accountability and allows members to benefit from the insights of other participants as they process the material they have studied during the week. The small groups also help build relationships as participants share prayer concerns and pray together. In the large-group time, members watch weekly video presentations in which Beth Moore enhances the material in the book and concludes each session with additional truths and challenges.

GROUP-SESSION FORMAT

For members to receive the greatest possible benefit from this study, plan for a 2-hour group session each week, plus a 15-minute check-in period. Following this format ensures that members receive the blessings of intimate experiences with God through daily study, support and fellowship through small-group discussions,

and inspiration through the video presentations. The session-leadership suggestions in this guide reflect the following schedule, although times shown here are arbitrary examples.

8:45 Child care open, attendance and homework check (15 min.)

9:00 Large group—welcome, worship, and prayer (15 min.)

9:15 Small groups (45 min.)
- Prayer (5 min.)
- Discussion of Principal Questions (20 min.)
- Discussion of Personal Discussion Questions (20 min.)

10:00 Break and return to large group (5 min.)

10:05 Large group (55 min.)
- Video presentation (50 min.)
- Closing assignment and prayer (5 min.)

11:00 Dismiss

This schedule is ideal for a weekday or a weeknight study. It may also be followed for the church's Discipleship Training period if the study is begun an hour earlier and does not interfere with other church activities.

Some elements of this format may be adjusted to your preferences or needs. For example, you may prefer to add time for a longer break between the small- and large-group periods. Feel free to adjust the schedule, but we encourage you not to omit any one of the three key ingredients of this learning model:
(1) individual study of the member book at home,
(2) small-group discussion of the Principal Questions and the Personal Discussion Questions in each week's material in the member book, and
(3) large-group viewing of the videos.

Here is an overview of the procedures for each segment of the group session.

Child care open, attendance and homework check (15 min.). Allow time for mothers to leave their children in child-care facilities prior to the session. Each participant must check in outside the large-group meeting room and have homework reviewed by the small-group facilitator. The facilitator does not check for correct responses but simply verifies that work is complete.

Large group—welcome, worship, and prayer (15 min.). The large-group leader is responsible for convening the group and conducting this portion of the session. You may wish to plan special music or select an appropriate hymn or praise song for the group to sing. End this segment with prayer for the day's learning experience.

Small-group discussion (45 min.). If the number of participants is small, remain in one group for this segment. If you enroll more than 12 people, however, plan for a small group for every 10 to 12 people and enlist a small-group facilitator for each group. These facilitators are responsible for taking prayer requests, having a prayer time (5 min.), and guiding participants to discuss the Principal Questions (20 min.) and Personal Discussion Questions (20 min.) in each week's material in the member book.

Return to large group (5 min.). This transitional time allows time for a brief break. Provide light refreshments if desired.

Video presentation (50 min.). A video presentation by Beth Moore is provided in the leader kit for each week's group session. The large-group leader should play the appropriate video at this time. Participants complete the corresponding video response sheet at the end of each week's material in their member books as they view the video. Beth concludes each video segment with a personal word and an additional challenge.

Closing assignment and prayer (5 min.). The large-group leader encourages participants to complete the next week's daily assignments and closes with a prayer of praise or thanksgiving.

OPTIONAL FORMAT

A format of meeting for an introductory session plus 2 hours per week for 10 weeks is ideal for studying *Jesus the One and Only;* however, you may need to seek another option to fit your group's situation. Many groups study these materials with an alternate schedule. The problem with studying on a schedule other than one unit per week is that members do not get into the regular habit of daily Bible study.

If you adopt an alternate plan, please take steps to encourage members to study the Bible daily. If your group can meet for only one hour per week, consider viewing the video one week and conducting the group study the next. To maintain the continuity of daily study, encourage members to complete the daily work in the member book during the first week. Then encourage them to review the work daily during the second week. Ask them to write down their answers to the Principal

Questions and Personal Discussion Questions each day during their review.

Some groups meet once a month. If your group meets on some schedule other than weekly or bi-weekly, consider using an aid to encourage daily Bible study. One such resource is called *Day by Day in God's Kingdom.* It is a discipleship journal built around six Christian disciplines. It allows disciples to record their spiritual journeys as they study courses such as *Jesus the One and Only.* Ask your members to complete the work in *Jesus the One and Only* during the first week of the study and to review the material the week before the group meets.

RESOURCES

The following resources are available.

- *Jesus the One and Only* (member book) provides an introduction and 10 weeks of daily, biblical studies on the life of Jesus. The book also includes viewer guides for video segments. Each participant needs a copy of the member book. Item 001116514
- *Jesus the One and Only Leader Kit* contains one copy of the member book; this leader guide; and six DVDs including an Introductory Session and Promotional Segments and featuring 10 lectures in which Beth Moore teaches material related to the content of the book. These videos are provided in the leader kit on DVDs and are available for download at *www.lifeway.com/women.*
- *Jesus the One and Only Leader Guide* (the guide you are now reading) offers step-by-step directions for facilitating 11 group sessions, using *Jesus the One and Only* member book and the videos included in the leader kit. This guide, one copy of which is included in the leader kit, is available separately. Item 001116515
- *Jesus the One and Only Audio CD Collection* includes the audio portions of Beth Moore's video presentations on 6 CDs, with a printable listening guide in PDF format. Although the CDs are designed for individual study, a leader may wish to use them for personal review and inspiration. Item 001288953

You will also need the following materials.

- Registration tables
- Small signs that indicate divisions of the alphabet— A–E, F–J, K–O, P–S, T–Z, for example.
- Registration cards
- An attendance sheet for each small-group facilitator
- Name tags and pencils
- Bibles
- A DVD player and monitor

CHOOSING LEADERS

The following are descriptions of the roles and responsibilities of leaders.

Large-group leader. This leader is not a teacher but an organizer, coordinator, and facilitator. The large-group leader's responsibilities include—

- providing administrative leadership for the group;
- scheduling the study;
- promoting the study and coordinating enrollment efforts;
- enlisting and coordinating the work of small-group facilitators;
- ordering and distributing resources;
- maintaining and submitting accurate records of participation each week as Discipleship Training attendance;
- leading the large-group segments of the weekly group sessions.

The large-group leader should be someone who is interested in exploring the crucial truths of this course and who desires to help others grow in intimacy with God. A long list of qualifications and years of teaching experience are not required. A heart prepared by God—being available and teachable—is more important. Paramount to this leader's success is a strong commitment to the study of this course and a faithful fulfillment of the basic responsibilities of group leadership.

This leader guide provides the large-group leader administrative help for organizing a Bible study group. It also gives specific guidance to prepare for and lead 11 group sessions.

Small-group facilitators. Enlist a small-group facilitator for every 10 to 12 participants. Again, these are not teachers but facilitators of the small groups' discussion and fellowship. Their responsibilities include—

- greeting and registering participants at the introductory session;
- calling members assigned to their small groups after the introductory session to introduce themselves, to tell them the locations of their small-group meeting rooms, and to encourage them to complete the daily assignments in week 1 of the member book;
- checking small-group members' attendance and homework prior to each week's meeting;
- taking prayer requests, conducting a prayer time at the beginning of the small-group period, praying for participants, and encouraging participants to pray for one another;
- guiding members to discuss the Principal Questions (listed at the beginning of each week's material in the member book) and the Personal Discussion Questions (designated by the dove symbol 🕊 in the member book);
- promoting fellowship among group members;
- noting opportunities for follow-up ministry.

If you have 12 or fewer participants, one leader can serve both the large- and small-group function. Each session of this guide designates the point during the session when small-group discussion is to occur. Share with each small-group facilitator a list of responsibilities and the following information about facilitating and handling problems in small groups.

FACILITATING SMALL-GROUP DISCUSSION

You will find many applications in this study for a contemporary walk with God. Beth Moore applies many of the course's concepts in her video presentations. In addition, the member book encourages participants to apply what they are learning as they complete their daily assignments.

One purpose of the small-group discussion period each week is to enable members to make meaningful application to their daily lives. Small-group facilitators will guide discussions of each week's Principal Questions, listed at the beginning of each week's material in the member book, as well as the Personal Discussion Questions. Small-group facilitators can use the following guidelines to make these discussion times effective in challenging participants spiritually and promoting life change.

- Arrange the chairs in the meeting room in a circle or a semicircle so that participants can see one another. Seating should not physically exclude anyone.
- Greet members as they arrive. Start the meeting on time. Allow 5 minutes for prayer requests; then pray or ask a participant to pray. Make notes when prayer requests are shared. Assure members that you are concerned not only about their spiritual growth but also about their personal lives. Encourage them to pray for one another during the week.
- If someone is experiencing difficult circumstances, write a note or call between sessions to say that you are praying for them.
- Spend 20 minutes discussing the week's Principal Questions (listed at the beginning of the week's material in the member book) and 20 minutes discussing Personal Discussion Questions (designated by the dove symbol 🕊 in the member book).

Emphasize that only participants who wish to respond should do so; no one is required to share responses. Do not force the discussion questions on members. Adapt and change them as necessary. Be flexible if members wish to spend more time on one group of questions or if they raise specific issues. Be sensitive to members' particular needs as the discussion progresses. Remember that your job is not to teach the material but to encourage and lead participants in sharing their insights about the work they have done during the week and in applying the content to their spiritual journeys.

- Be personally involved without relinquishing leadership. Your role as facilitator is that of a fellow disciple—one who shares the same struggles the other participants have in their spiritual lives. You need to be emotionally vulnerable and willing to share some of your own feelings and responses. However, you must also recognize that someone must lead the group and direct the discussion at all times. Be flexible, but do not allow the discussion to veer off on a tangent. Keep the focus on the week's content and its application.

- Try to create a relaxed atmosphere that will help every member feel a sense of belonging. Use first names. Do not rush the discussion.

- Pray for the Holy Spirit's leadership; then allow Him freedom to direct the session as He wills. His movement may be evident in tears of joy or conviction, emotional or spiritual brokenness, or the thrill of a newfound insight. Be sensitive to signs of God's work in a person's life and follow up by asking the person to share. Giving participants the opportunity to testify to what God is doing is very important. Often, the testimony may help another person with a similar issue. Follow the Holy Spirit's leadership as God works in these discussion times.

- Be sure that you do not talk too much as facilitator. Do not be afraid of periods of silence.

- Be an encourager. Show a caring, loving spirit. Communicate acceptance and concern, especially if your group includes non-Christians. Create an atmosphere that communicates, "I accept you as you are." Accepting participants does not necessarily mean that you agree with their values or choices. You can love a person without agreeing with that person. If a participant shares something that makes her feel vulnerable or ashamed, say something like: "I know your sharing took a lot of courage. I admire you for being willing to share it."

- Listen intently and aggressively. When someone shares something personal or painful, lean toward her. Use facial expressions to show concern. Nod your head.

- Be ready to address special needs that members may reveal. If someone is unsaved, follow the Holy Spirit's leadership to know the right time to talk with the person privately to lead her to Christ. If a participant reveals emotional pain or family problems, assure her of the group's concern and support and pause briefly to pray with the person. Then offer to meet with her later to help her find additional help if needed.

- Set boundaries. Do not permit a group member to act in a verbally abusive way toward another member. Do not force group members to do or say anything they are not willing to do or say. Try gently nudging a group member to a point of discovery and growth instead of pushing her to a conclusion for which she is not ready.

- Be enthusiastic!

- End the discussion period on time. You will face a challenge each week in bringing the discussion to an end in time for members to have a five-minute break before the large group reconvenes. At the first session emphasize the need to conclude on time each week. A few minutes before time to end the discussion period, help the person speaking reach a point of closure. Ask if anyone has anything to add. Allow response, then at some point end the discussion. If someone is not finished, affirm the importance of what the person is saying. Offer to continue the discussion next week and ask that member to introduce the topic at the beginning of the next meeting. Or you may need to spend time privately with the person if the topic does not relate to the entire group. Be sure you have tied loose ends. Did you put someone on hold during the discussion? Did you get back to the person? Was someone's sharing interrupted as you moved to focus on someone else's response? Did you reach closure with the original speaker? Finally, remind group members to pray for one another during the week.

COPING WITH PROBLEMS IN THE SMALL GROUP
No matter how meaningful the study and how effective the leadership, difficulties can arise in any group. Following are common problems and suggestions for dealing with them.

Absenteeism. Absentees miss a potentially life-changing experience and diminish others' learning. If a participant is absent, contact the person, communicate your concern, and encourage her to make up the work. Otherwise, a participant will quickly get further behind and likely drop out.

● *Not completing at-home assignments.* Emphasize in the introductory session that a significant course requirement is doing daily study at home, including completion of the learning activities. State that each person's book will be checked before each session to see that homework was completed. Anyone unwilling to make this commitment should not participate in the study.

If someone has not completed the week's assignments, encourage the person to stay up-to-date to gain the greatest benefits from the study. If someone continually refuses to complete the assignments, meet with her and suggest that she withdraw and participate at a time when she can devote herself adequately to the study.

Disagreement with the content. Some debate in a group is productive. Remember that the Scriptures should always be the final source of authority. If debate becomes counterproductive, suggest that you and the participant discuss the matter later so other members can participate in the present discussion.

Do not feel threatened if someone expects you to be an authority and to answer all of her questions. Emphasize your role as the facilitator of the discussion, pointing out that participants are to learn from one another and that you are not an authority on the subject. Suggest that a volunteer research the question during the week and report at the next meeting if the person insists that an answer is important to her.

A participant who dominates the group. Ways a person may dominate a group are—

- claiming a major portion of each discussion period to talk about her issues;
- repeatedly waiting until the last 10 minutes of a meeting to introduce an emotionally charged story or problem;
- attempting to block other group members' sharing;
- judging others' behavior or confessions;
- challenging your leadership in a hostile way;
- criticizing other group members' motives or feelings.

As the facilitator, make sure every person has an opportunity to share. Discourage dominating members by calling on others, by asking someone to speak who has not yet responded, or by focusing directly on someone else. If these methods do not work, talk privately with the dominating person and enlist the person's support in involving everyone in future discussions.

When a person is going into too much detail and is losing the attention of the group, you will usually notice that the group has disconnected. Direct the sharing back on course by discreetly interrupting the person and by restating the point she is trying to make: "So what you are saying is …." Another method is to interrupt and restate the question you asked originally: "And Liz, what did you learn about God's love through that experience?" Even if the speaker is somewhat unsettled by this response, she should respond by restating the response more succinctly.

PLANNING STEPS

The following steps are suggestioons that will assist the large-group leader in organizing a study of *Jesus the One and Only.*

1. Enlist the support of your pastor. His endorsement will encourage people to deepen their spiritual lives. Perhaps he will agree to announce from the pulpit this discipleship opportunity.

2. Talk with the likely participants to determine the level of interest in this type of in-depth study. Ask whether the study should be offered during the day, in the evening, or both. When scheduling the study, be sensitive to the needs of women who work outside the home.

3. Schedule 11 weeks on the church calender that will allow the greatest participation. Fall and spring studies usually result in more participation than summer sessions do. However, summertime may afford some persons with seasonal careers—such as schoolteachers—an opportunity to attend an intimate discipleship study.

4. Offer child care if possible. This will increase your attendance and ensure greater weekly participation.

5. Allow two hours for each weekly session. This time period will allow ample opportunities for both weekly activities: small-group discussion of the participants' home study and large-group viewing of the week's video presentation.

6. After estimating the number of participants, order member books (*Jesus the One and Only*, Item 001116514) between four and six weeks in advance. WRITE to LifeWay Church Resources Customer Service; One LifeWay Plaza; Nashville, TN 37234-0113; FAX order to (615) 251-5933; PHONE (800) 458-2772; EMAIL to *orderentry@lifeway.com;* ORDER ONLINE at *www.lifeway.com;* or VISIT the LifeWay

Christian Store serving you. Decide whether the church will pay for member books or whether participants will pay for their own. Experience has shown that if members pay for their books or a portion of the cost, they are likely to make a more serious commitment to the study. Make sure that scholarships are provided for members who cannot afford to purchase their own books.

7. Find a meeting room that will accommodate your large-group sessions and reserve it for the duration of the study. Reserve small-group meeting rooms for the number of groups you will have. Arrange the meeting rooms to be as intimate as possible. Chairs in the small-group rooms should be arranged in circles or semicircles. Semicircular rows of chairs are acceptable for the large-group room as long as all participants can view the video.

8. Conduct a planning session for the large-group leader and the small-group facilitators. Complete the following actions in the meeting.
   • Obtain copies of this leader guide for your small-group facilitators. Discuss the group-session format and their responsibilities, which include:
     —greeting and registering participants at the introductory session;
     —calling members assigned to their small groups after the introductory session to introduce themselves, explain the locations of their small-group meeting rooms, and encourage them to complete the daily assignments for week 1;
     —checking small-group members' attendance and homework prior to each week's meeting;
     —taking prayer requests, conducting a prayer time at the beginning of the small-group period, praying for participants, and encouraging participants to pray for one another;
     —guiding members to discuss the Principal Questions (listed at the beginning of each week's material in the member book) and the Personal Discussion Questions;
     —promoting fellowship among group members;
     —noting opportunities for follow-up ministry.
   • Discuss registration procedures. Plan to set up several registration tables outside the large-group meeting room with signs indicating divisions of the alphabet. For example, participants whose last names begin with A–E will register at one station, F–J at the next, K–O at the next, P–S at the next, and T–Z at the final station. Assign small-group facilitators to handle registration at the stations.

The members registered by a particular facilitator would become members of her group. Make adjustments if numbers fall unevenly. Instruct the facilitators to be at their stations 30 minutes before registration begins at the introductory session. Provide them with a supply of member books, registration cards, pencils, and reusable name tags. Tell each registrar that she has the responsibility of making a good first impression. She needs to wear a name tag, greet members with enthusiasm, answer their questions as best she can or promise to find out the answers, make them feel welcome, and direct them to the large-group session. At subsequent sessions the small-group facilitators will follow the same procedures to check attendance and homework.

   • Explain that after the introductory session small-group facilitators will transfer names from their registration cards to attendance sheets that you will provide. Each week they will record attendance, completion of homework, and prayer requests on this sheet. Emphasize that facilitators are merely to check whether participants have responded to the learning activities in the member book, not to determine whether responses are correct.

9. Promote the study, using the suggestions in the following section.

10. Plan to keep accurate records and report attendance to the church office. Regardless of when the study is offered, it is a Discipleship Training study and should be reported as Discipleship Training participation on the Annual Church Profile. Another reason to keep accurate participation records is that participants can earn Christian Growth Study Plan diplomas for completing the study. For details see the requirements on page 239 of the member book.

11. Pray, pray, and keep praying that God will involve the members He desires and that He will validate this study with His obvious presence and activity!

PROMOTING THE STUDY

This study provides a wonderful opportunity for outreach because it is free of rules and does not require a particular church affiliation. Target persons in your community who are interested in Bible study. Church bulletins, newsletters, handouts, posters, fliers at Mothers' Day Out, announcements in worship services and in Sunday School classes, phone calls, and word of mouth are excellent and inexpensive ways to promote the study. Sometimes local radio and television stations announce upcoming events free of charge.

To assist you in promoting the study, we have provided two special promotional segments on DVD 1 included in the leader kit. You may want to preview them now. You will find them immediately before the introductory session. The first segment has been designed for your use inside the church—in a worship service, in a women's Bible study class, and in other locations where women regularly gather during the week. You have permission to duplicate this segment if you wish to create a loop tape that plays continually. Be sure to have someone prepared to announce the date, time, and place of the introductory session and to invite persons to attend. If the tape is left to play unattended, place a sign beside the monitor that lists the date, time, and place of the introductory session.

ADJUSTING FOR THE CHURCH CALENDAR

Some churches prefer to run their Bible-study groups in regular 13-week cycles. If you wish to plan this study for 13 weeks, the following suggestions will enable you to fit the study into such a schedule.

1. The first week: conduct an opening/orientation. If you have multiple groups, overview all the different groups that may be meeting simultaneously, or just overview *Jesus the One and Only*. Include testimonies from a previous Bible study. Possibly include refreshments or a brown-bag meal.

2. The second week: use the introductory session plan on page 10 of this guide.

3. On weeks 3 through 12 do the study as outlined in the following pages.

4. On week 13 have a closing celebration with testimonies of changed lives through this study. Share a pot-luck meal together. Award certificates to participants. Close with a prayer of commitment.

Use your own creativity to plan a schedule for this Bible study that will permit the maximum participation and opportunity for growth. As you pray and work, the Holy Spirit will lead you to a plan that is right for your church and ministry.

Notes

Introductory Session

GOALS FOR THIS SESSION

In this session you will—

- register all members for *Jesus the One and Only;*
- develop a role or attendance sheet;
- distribute member books;
- explain basics about the format;
- view introductory video presentation.

BEFORE THE SESSION

1. If you are expecting 20 or more participants, set up tables with cards indicating a division of the alphabet at several stations. For example, those with last names beginning with letters A–E will sign up at one station, F–J at the next, and so forth.

2. Enlist a volunteer or group leader to sit at each station. One way of distributing members to groups is to designate those each leader registers as members of her group. Adjustments will need to be made where numbers fall unevenly.

3. Each "registrar," whether leader or volunteer, should be at her station 30 minutes before registration is to begin. Each should be equipped with member books, registration cards, or sign-up sheets (drawn up by your church or study leader), pens, and name tags.

4. Each registrar assumes the responsibility for the first impression of each new member. She needs to wear her name tag, be ready to greet new members with enthusiasm, anticipate questions with knowledgeable answers, make participants feel welcome, and tell them what to do next. (After registration, members will report to the joint session for the introductory segment. After this first introductory meeting, members will begin each week in their large groups for welcome, worship, and prayer.)

DURING THE SESSION

Introduction to *Jesus the One and Only* (60 min.)

1. Open introductory session in prayer.

2. Welcome members and introduce leaders. If your group is small, you might have each member introduce herself. You may want to create your own icebreaker to help introduce members to one another.

3. After introductions, give instructions and information concerning the course. Include the following and any additional points pertinent to your church facility:

A. Have members scan the first week's daily assignments. Make sure they understand to complete a week of study prior to each weekly meeting. Before the next meeting, complete week 1. Make sure they understand that, although the daily assignments are crucial, members are urged to attend the weekly sessions even if their work is incomplete. Tell them to expect each daily assignment to take approximately 30–45 minutes.

B. Encourage members to read the introduction in the member book before beginning their study.

C. Using the introduction to the member book, explain that the format is designed to enhance learning. Point out that the Principal Questions, listed in the introduction to each unit, and the Personal Discussion Questions, appearing with the dove symbol 🕊, will be discussed in the weekly group sessions.

D. Emphasize the primary reasons for small-group discussion are:
- accountability—in-depth Bible studies are most often completed successfully in a group.
- to underscore basic biblical truths. This will be accomplished through discussing answers to the Principal Questions, which insure that the biblical information offered in the study has been received and understood.
- to personally apply the study. This will be accomplished through discussing answers to the Personal Discussion Questions.

E. Express the need to be good stewards of the time for each session. The way time is organized can mean the success or failure of any group. Ask participants to adopt the following time guidelines.
- Leaders: Be early!
- Members: Be on time!
- Small groups: Start on time! Leaders must make a habit from the beginning to start on time regardless of the number present.
- Members: Your personal comments are vital to the discussion time, but please make them brief to make the class run smoothly.

4. After today's introductory meeting, members will participate in a small group each week as well as a large group. (Tell them they will receive a phone call

within 24 hours identifying their leader and telling where their group will meet for discussion of sessions 1–10). Allow 45 minutes for small-group discussion divided according to the following schedule.

- Prayer requests and prayer (5 min.). If you ask for prayer requests, ask that they be stated in one brief sentence. Be prepared to graciously intervene if a request becomes lengthy.
- Discussion of Principal Questions and Personal Discussion Questions (40 min.). Allow 7–8 minutes to discuss each day's assignment. Each day's Principal Question can be answered in 2–3 minutes, leaving 5–6 minutes for Personal Discussion Question. Write these time divisions on a chalkboard for all members to keep in mind and be dedicated to enforcing them.

Introductory Video Presentation (50 min.)
Each week after the group discussion, gather members in joint session to view the video that enhances and concludes each unit. Take 5 minutes for the transition. The video presentation will be 45–50 minutes.

Closing Remarks and Prayer (5 min.)
1. After viewing the video, share any closing comments. Give a brief introduction to the next unit. This introduction may be as simple as saying, "Next week our study is entitled, The Word Made Flesh."
2. Answer any questions, or if you do not know the answer, call the questioner as soon as you have the information she desires. Don't forget to take up name tags as the group departs.

AFTER THE SESSION
1. Compile all registration cards and, if there are more than 12 members and more than 1 leader, divide the list of members into small groups. These discussion groups need to be a maximum of 12 members.
2. Have leader(s) call members within the next 24 hours to introduce themselves and tell them where their group will meet the following week.
3. Have a leader or volunteer create attendance sheets from the registration cards so that every leader will be able to take roll of her individual group at each of the next 10 sessions. These attendance sheets need to be given to each leader prior to the next session.

I know you can do it. If you follow these guidelines you will have no problem being good stewards of the time period. You can help insure learners are receiving the

utmost from this study by implementing the suggestions you've received through this introduction.

God's Word changes lives! If a woman dedicates herself to the hours in God's Word this study will require, her life will undoubtedly be transformed. As a leader, be careful not to let your administration of this study eclipse your participation. Open God's Word and enjoy!

JUST BETWEEN US

My heart is so tender and full of gratitude toward those God has raised to facilitate these Bible studies. I cannot imagine how I could be so blessed to work with you.

If you're thinking you're not up to this challenge, I know exactly how you feel! I can't think of a thing God has ever appointed me to do that wasn't completely beyond me. What helps me most when I feel overwhelmed is remembering that none of this is about me! It's all about Him. How I do is not the issue. You and I will do just fine as long as our occasional bouts with doubts are limited to ourselves and not extended to Him.

Keep in mind that the most wonderful and effective leader is the close follower of Christ. We want to be such followers of Christ that when our leadership is complete, we can step out of the way, and our flock will keep following Christ, not us!

Fanning the flames of your own intimate relationship with Christ is the most critical practice in leadership. Don't get so busy leading Bible study that you don't get your homework completed. I ask you to covenant with me right now that your priority plan will be to enjoy God and passionately pursue His Son throughout this journey. Then, even if you have trouble finding the "play" button on the DVD player, you'll still be a wonderful leader!

I want to challenge you to complete one lesson ahead of time. Before you start week 1, day 1, please complete week 6, day 5 (pp. 141-145). Use an extra sheet of paper for your answers so you can do the lesson again, when you and your group reach week 6. I believe the lesson has the potential to dramatically impact your approach to leadership.

Dear One, thank you so much for your willingness to lead others to know and to love Jesus Christ. He is not just the most important thing in life. He is life. Have a blast with Him.

SESSION 1
The Word Made Flesh

BEFORE THE SESSION
1. Complete all of week 1 in the member book.
2. Pause and pray for each member of your group by name. Pray specifically that each will be teachable and that God will reveal Himself through this study.
3. Pray for God's guidance in your preparation for this week's group session.
4. Carefully read through "During the Session" and be sure you are prepared for each question and activity that will take place at this week's group session.
5. Arrange your room to meet the needs of your group. An intimate setting seems to be most beneficial. If you have a group of 12 or under, arrange the chairs in a tight circle. If you have more than 12, two tight semi-circles will work well.
6. If you are using the video, do the following:
   • Make sure all arrangements have been made to secure and set up necessary equipment.
   • If you have more than one small group, the arrangements need to be made in one room for the joint session. If you have only one group, the arrangements will be made in the room where the discussion group meets.
   • Preview the video and fill in your viewing guide. This step will be beneficial to you in case you are detained or distracted with administrative duties as the members watch the video.
   • Prepare several sentences, based on your response to the video, from which you can make closing remarks at the end of class just prior to dismissal.

Child Care Open, Attendance and Homework Check (15 min.)

DURING THE SESSION
Large Group—Welcome, Worship, and Prayer (15 min.)
1. Greet each member as she arrives and give her the name tag she used in the introductory session. Learn to call every participant by name.
2. Lead a time of worship and praise.
3. Pray, asking for God's presence and blessing throughout the session.
4. Dismiss to small groups.

Small Groups (45 min.)
1. Ask for prayer requests and have prayer (5 min.).
2. Review the week's Principal Questions and Personal Discussion Questions (40 min.).

Look for brief and basic answers to the Principal Questions just so you can be satisfied that the material was received and understood. Two to three minutes should be sufficient. All answers should be obvious as the reading and the learning activities of week 1 are performed and completed; however, make sure that you have written basic answers to the questions so that you can supply the information if a member does not volunteer or understand the answer.

Each day's Principal Question will be followed by a Personal Discussion Question. Personal Discussion Questions are identified in each day's study by the dove symbol. Anyone may share their answers to the Personal Discussion Questions. Do not pressure group members to share their answers. Give them the opportunity if they wish. Please ask them always to be discreet and never to name another person who could be hurt by the discussion. Appropriate discussion of these questions will be invaluable to the application of the session. Leader, you must be ready and willing to redirect discussion if at any point it becomes inappropriate. Please pray for discretion and boldness on your part.

Day 1:
• *Principal Question:* Based on Luke 1:18-25, how did Zechariah receive Gabriel's news?
• *Personal Discussion:* What long-standing prayer request have you continued to take to God's throne?

Day 2:
• *Principal Question:* Matthew 2:23 records an oral prophecy handed down through the generations. What was the prophecy?
• *Personal Discussion:* What would be a question you would want to ask the earthly mom of the infant Christ if you ever get the chance in heaven?

Day 3:
• *Principal Question:* Based on Luke 1:39-56, what did Mary do after receiving Gabriel's news?

• *Personal Discussion:* When was the last time you were stunned by something God did for you and perhaps wondered, "Who am I that You would even look upon me?"

Day 4:
• *Principal Question:* According to Luke 1:78 why did God enact His intricate, redemptive plan?
• *Personal Discussion:* Where do you see yourself in Zechariah's words of prophecy? In other words, which parts pertain to you or have been fulfilled in your life?

Day 5:
• *Principal Question:* What two responses did Mary have to all the events that followed Christ's birth?
• *Personal Discussion:* What is your favorite part of the Christmas story?

If time allows, ask what ways God spoke directly to members in week 1.

Conclude 40-minute discussion time by thanking members for their willingness to share and affirming their apparent grasp of the material. If you are using the optional video, it is time to move into large group to view the video or turn on the video in the one small group. If you are not viewing the video, you may dismiss with a few introductory words about week 2 and a closing prayer at this time. Take the 5 remaining minutes in the first hour to prepare for the video.

Break and Return to Large Group (5 min.)

View the Video Presentation (50 min.)

Conclude Session (5 min.)
• Leader gives a brief response to the video in one or two sentences.
• Leader gives a brief introduction to week 2 in her own words and encourages them to complete the next week's study before the next session.
• Leader closes with prayer. This would not be the time to take prayer requests. That opportunity was given at the beginning of the small-group session.
• Leader takes up name tags as group departs.

If you were able to abide by your time schedule, you will be able to dismiss on time. However, satisfy any unexpected but brief needs or comments that arise.

AFTER THE SESSION

1. Immediately record any concerns or impressions you had to pray for any member in your group while it is still fresh on your mind. Remember to pray for these throughout the week.
2. Evaluate session 1 by asking yourself the following questions and recording your answers:
   • Was I adequately prepared for today's session?
   • Was I able to begin and end session 1 on time?
   • If not, how can I help to make sure our time is used more wisely in session 2?
   • Do any members need extra encouragement this week? Note whether a card or a phone call would be appropriate; then remember to follow up on each one.
   • What was my overall impression of session 1?
3. Read through "Before the Session" on page 12 so that you will know what preparations you'll need to make before your next session.
4. Have lunch with a friend, stop for a soft drink, have a cup of hot chocolate, or make time for a nap. Treat yourself to a moment's recreation for the work you've allowed God to accomplish through you!

JUST BETWEEN US

Whew! The first week is behind you! That's usually the hardest one. I wish I could be there with you to clean up the room and put everything back in its place. We'd get down on our knees together right in that room and thank God for what He did even if we weren't satisfied with what we did. I tell you what, I'll just get down on my knees right here and you get down on your knees right there and let's pray as if we were side-by-side.

Father, we thank You for the promise that Your Word has a written guarantee. It cannot return void. You have ordained a purpose for every single person in this group. You have even ordained the size of the group. We do not know why You have chosen to place us in these positions but we thank You. You do not make mistakes. We are so humbled that You would allow us to join You in Your work. If we can be used by You to encourage others to know and love You more, we are blessed indeed. Meet every member of this group on the pages of Your powerful Word this week. We love You, Jesus. Be our One and Only. Amen.

SESSION 2
The Son of God

BEFORE THE SESSION
Refer to page 12 for a description of session procedures.

Child Care Open, Attendance and Homework Check (15 min.)

DURING THE SESSION
Large Group—Welcome, Worship, and Prayer (15 min.)
1. Greet each member as she arrives and give her the name tag she used in the introductory session. Learn to call every participant by name.
2. Lead a time of worship and praise.
3. Pray, asking for God's presence and blessing throughout the session.
4. Dismiss to small groups.

Small Groups (45 min.)
1. Ask for prayer requests and have prayer (5 min.).
2. Review the week's Principal Questions and Personal Discussion Questions (40 min.).

Remember, Leader, you are looking for brief and basic answers to the Principal Questions that will indicate the comprehension of the reading and learning activities in week 2. Again, make sure that you are prepared to offer the answer in the event that a member does not volunteer. Also, be prepared to keep personal discussion within appropriate bounds.

Day 1:
- *Principal Question:* According to Isaiah 49:6, why was Christ not sent for the nation of Israel alone?
- *Personal Discussion:* How should our spiritual circumcision offer proof that we are different than the persons we originally were?

Day 2:
- *Principal Question:* What are some of the inferences in Matthew 13:54-58 regarding a typical home life for Christ?
- *Personal Discussion:* How does asking questions of God differ from questioning God?

Day 3:
- *Principal Question:* What does Isaiah 53:2 tell us about Christ's physical appearance?
- *Personal Discussion:* What characteristics of people tend to capture your favor?

Day 4:
- *Principal Question:* If you were doing a character study on Satan (from Luke 4:1-13), what could you learn about him?
- *Personal Discussion:* What do you think "putting God to the test" means?

Day 5:
- *Principal Question:* Based on a comparison of Luke 4:18-19 and Isaiah 61:1-2, what are the phrases that detail Christ's God-given job description?
- *Personal Discussion:* Based on Christ's job description, what would have been a good name for His ministry?

If time allows, ask what ways God spoke directly to members in week 2.

Conclude the 40-minute discussion time by affirming your members in their participation today and their apparent grasp of the material. If you are using the video, move into large group to view the video or turn on the video in the one small group. If you are not viewing the video, you may dismiss with a few introductory words about week 3 and a closing prayer.

Break and Return to Large Group (5 min.)

View the Video Presentation (50 min.)

Conclude Session (5 min.)
- Leader gives a brief response to the video in one or two sentences.
- Leader gives a brief introduction to week 3 in her own words and encourages them toward the completion of their home study.
- Leader closes with prayer. Again, prayer requests will not be necessary since they were taken at the beginning of discussion.
- Leader takes up name tags as group departs.

AFTER THE SESSION

1. Immediately record any concerns or impressions you had to pray for any member in your group while it is still fresh on your mind. Remember to pray for these throughout the week.

2. Evaluate session 2 by asking yourself the following questions. Be sure to record your answers.
   - Was I adequately prepared for today's session?
   - Was I able to begin and end session 2 on time? If not, how can I make sure our time is used more wisely in session 3?
   - Are there any members who may need extra encouragement this week? Note whether a card or phone call would be appropriate; then remember to follow up on each one.
   - What was my overall impression of session 2?

3. Read through "Before the Session" on page 12 so that you will know what preparations you'll need to make before your next session.

JUST BETWEEN US

Two weeks behind you! Are you beginning to see any fruit among the people in your group? Nothing thrills me more than watching a "light go on" for someone in my group. I want nothing more in ministry than for others to know Jesus and hear Him for themselves! I am praying that God will grant you the unspeakable blessing of watching the scales fall away from the eyes of those in your group so that you may behold them beholding Him. Hallelujah!

You are off to a great start. Remember, Christ is both the Author and Finisher of every assignment He entrusts to you. He has begun a good work and He will complete it. If no one else changes a bit, and they will, may you and I both be more like Him when He completes His work in our study.

Notes

_____

_____

_____

_____

_____

_____

_____

_____

_____

_____

_____

_____

_____

_____

SESSION 3
The Way and Life

BEFORE THE SESSION

Refer to page 12 for a description of session procedures.

Child Care Open, Attendance and Homework Check (15 min.)

DURING THE SESSION

Large Group—Welcome, Worship, and Prayer (15 min.)

1. Greet each member as she arrives and give her the name tag she used in the introductory session. Learn to call every participant by name.
2. Lead a time of worship and praise.
3. Pray, asking for God's presence and blessing throughout the session.
4. Dismiss to small groups.

Small Groups (45 min.)

1. Ask for prayer requests and have prayer (5 min.).
2. Review the week's Principal Questions and Personal Discussion Questions (40 min.).

Day 1:
- *Principal Question:* What is your understanding of the events in Luke 4:22-30? How did the crowd's mood change when Christ confronted them?
- *Personal Discussion:* What do you think would have been the manner of ministry the synagogue leaders expected?

Day 2:
- *Principal Question:* Why do you think healing the sick was not the absolute priority work Christ came to accomplish?
- *Personal Discussion:* Has Christ's activity in your home come about as a direct result of some threatening situation?

Day 3:
- *Principal Question:* What conclusions can you draw from the kinds of people Christ called to do things His way?
- *Personal Discussion:* Why do you think Simon Peter suddenly fell at Jesus' knees and said, "Go away from me, Lord; I am a sinful man!" (Luke 5:8)?

Day 4:
- *Principal Question:* How did Jesus see the faith of the paralytic and his friends (Luke 5:20)?
- *Personal Discussion:* How like the leper are you? Are you convinced that Christ can do absolutely anything, and are you also seeking His purposes in everything?

Day 5:
- *Principal Question:* Based on Luke 6:7, what were the Pharisees and teachers of the law looking for?
- *Personal Discussion:* How do you tend to make rest more work than work?

If time allows, ask what ways God spoke directly to members in week 3.

Conclude 40-minute discussion time by affirming your members in their participation today and their apparent grasp of the material. If you are using the optional video, move into large group to view the video or turn on the video in the one small group. If you are not viewing the video, you may dismiss with a few introductory words about week 4 and a closing prayer.

Break and Return to Large Group (5 min.)

View the Video Presentation (50 min.)

Conclude Session (5 min.)
- Leader gives a brief response to the video in one or two sentences.
- Leader gives a brief introduction to week 4 in her own words and encourages them toward the completion of their home study.
- Leader closes with prayer. Again, since prayer requests were taken at the beginning of discussion, they would not be necessary at this time.
- Leader takes up name tags as group departs.

AFTER THE SESSION

1. Immediately record any concerns or impressions you had to pray for any member in your group while it is still fresh on your mind. Remember to pray for these throughout the week.

2. Evaluate session 3 by asking yourself the following questions and recording your answers:
   - Was I adequately prepared for today's session?
   - Was I able to begin and end session 3 on time?
   - If not, how can I help to make sure our time is used more wisely in session 4?
   - Are there any members who may need extra encouragement this week? Note whether a card or phone call would be appropriate; then remember to follow up on each one.
   - What was my overall impression of session 3?
3. Read through "Before the Session" on page 12 so that you will know what preparations you'll need to make before your next session.

JUST BETWEEN US

Dear Leader, I hope so much that your group members are discovering treasure after treasure in their pursuit of Christ. How about you? In many ways, I consider you leaders my "group." I want to make sure you stay encouraged. Remember not to get so involved in facilitating that you miss the joy of discovering the treasures of Christ for yourself. Tell Him you don't want to miss a single gem He has for you. Ask Him to broaden your mind and deepen your heart, taking you to a place of intimacy with Him that you've never been. As others follow you, may they follow you straight to Christ! You are doing a fabulous job, Dear One. Persevere!

Notes

_____

_____

_____

_____

_____

_____

_____

_____

_____

_____

_____

SESSION 4
The Esteem of Man

BEFORE THE SESSION
Refer to page 12 for a description of session procedures.

Child Care Open, Attendance and Homework Check (15 min.)

DURING THE SESSION
Large Group—Welcome, Worship, and Prayer (15 min.)
1. Greet each member as she arrives and give her the name tag she used in the introductory session. Learn to call every participant by name.
2. Lead a time of worship and praise.
3. Pray, asking for God's presence and blessing throughout the session.
4. Dismiss to small groups.

Small Groups (45 min.)
1. Ask for prayer requests and have prayer (5 min.).
2. Review the week's Principal Questions and Personal Discussion Questions (40 min.).

Day 1:
• *Principal Question:* How did the centurion's occupation lend him insight into Christ's ability?
• *Personal Discussion:* How can you accurately conclude that you are precious?

Day 2:
• *Principal Question:* What differences can you identify between the two miracles recorded in Luke 7:1-17?
• *Personal Discussion:* What do we fellow humans usually mean when we say, "Don't cry"?

Day 3:
• *Principal Question:* According to Mark 6:17-18, why was John the Baptist in prison?
• *Personal Discussion:* Has God ever taken you through your doubts to a place of greater faith?

Day 4:
• *Principal Question:* Can you summarize, in one sentence, the parable Christ told the Pharisee in Luke 7:41-42?

• *Personal Discussion:* What does the woman's willingness to go to the Pharisee's house with her alabaster jar say about her?

Day 5:
• *Principal Question:* According to Luke 8:19-21, what was the sudden development in Christ's family dynamics?
• *Personal Discussion:* What can you imagine Mary felt when Jesus' "own brothers did not believe in him" (John 7:5)?

If time allows, ask what ways God spoke directly to members in week 4.

Conclude 40-minute discussion time by affirming your members in their participation today and their apparent grasp of the material. If you are using the optional video, move into large group to view the video or turn on the video in the one small group. If you are not viewing the video, you may dismiss with a few introductory words about week 5 and a closing prayer.

Break and Return to Large Group (5 min.)

View the Video Presentation (50 min.)

Conclude Session (5 min.)
• Leader gives a brief response to the video in one or two sentences.
• Leader gives a brief introduction to week 5 in her own words and encourages them toward the completion of their home study.
• Leader closes with prayer. Again, since prayer requests were taken at the beginning of discussion, they would not be necessary at this time.
• Leader takes up name tags as group departs.

AFTER THE SESSION
1. Immediately record any concerns or impressions you had to pray for any member in your group while it is still fresh on your mind. Remember to pray for these throughout the week.
2. Evaluate session 4 by asking yourself the following questions and recording your answers:
   • Was I adequately prepared for today's session?

- Was I able to begin and end session 4 on time?
- If not, how can I help to make sure our time is used more wisely in session 5?
- Do any members need extra encouragement this week? Note whether a card or phone call would be appropriate; then make a point to remember and follow up on each one.

- What was my overall impression of session 4?

3. Read through "Before the Session" on page 12 so that you will know what preparations you'll need to make before your next session.

JUST BETWEEN US

Do you have a little trouble imagining Christ being proud of you? Can you imagine our children not being able to believe we're proud of them? Go ahead. Believe it. God has appointed you to this realm of service and you have obeyed. The consequences are now entirely up to Him.

Obedience is one way Jesus says we demonstrate our love for Him. "Whoever has my commands and obeys them, he is the one who loves me" (John 14:21). Another way is to love those around us. "Love each other as I have loved you" (John 15:12). You are actively engaged in two profound expressions of love for God as you facilitate the flock God has entrusted to you. Yes, He's proud of you. Sit back and savor it for a moment.

Notes

_____

_____

_____

_____

_____

_____

_____

_____

_____

_____

_____

SESSION 5

The Christ of God

BEFORE THE SESSION
Refer to page 12 for a description of session procedures.

Child Care Open, Attendance and Homework Check (15 min.)

DURING THE SESSION
Large Group—Welcome, Worship, and Prayer (15 min.)
1. Greet each member and distribute name tags. Learn to call every participant by name.
2. Lead a time of worship and praise.
3. Pray, asking for God's presence and blessing throughout the session.
4. Dismiss to small groups.

Small Groups (45 min.)
1. Ask for prayer requests and have prayer (5 min.).
2. Review the week's Principal Questions and Personal Discussion Questions (40 min.).

Day 1:
- *Principal Question:* What "super-human" characteristics did the man have due to his demon possession?
- *Personal Discussion:* How can we know if our times of isolation are being used by God or by the enemy?

Day 2:
- *Principal Question:* Can you describe the peculiar swing in emotions in the people at Jairus' house?
- *Personal Discussion:* What analogy would you use to describe what Jesus felt when He felt the power "go out" from Him?

Day 3:
- *Principal Question:* According to Luke 9:1, what did Christ give the twelve to perform certain supernatural tasks?
- *Personal Discussion:* What are God's purposes in your life? What is your calling?

Day 4:
- *Principal Question:* What do you think Christ might have been testing in His disciples?

- *Personal Discussion:* When was the last time you saw Christ take the equivalent of a few fish and loaves and multiply them before your eyes?

Day 5:
- *Principal Question:* According to Matthew 16:21-23, what did Peter do after Christ announced His imminent suffering and death?
- *Personal Discussion:* When we are struggling, how can we stir the things of God in our thinking rather than the things of man?

If time allows, ask what ways God spoke directly to members in week 5.

Conclude 40-minute discussion time by affirming members in their participation today and their apparent grasp of the material. If you are using the optional video, move into large group to view the video or turn on the video in the one small group. If you are not viewing the video, you may dismiss with a few introductory words about week 6 and a closing prayer at this time.

Break and Return to Large Group (5 min.)

View the Video Presentation (50 min.)

Conclude Session (5 min.)
- Leader gives a brief response to the video in one or two sentences.
- Leader gives a brief introduction to week 6 in her own words and encourages them toward the completion of their home study.
- Leader closes with prayer. Again, since prayer requests were taken at the beginning of discussion, they would not be necessary at this time.
- Leader takes up name tags as group departs.

AFTER THE SESSION
1. Immediately record any concerns or impressions you had to pray for any member in your group while it is still fresh on your mind. Remember to pray for these throughout the week.
2. Evaluate session 5 by asking yourself the following questions and recording your answers:
   - Was I adequately prepared for today's session?

- Was I able to begin and end session 5 on time?
- If not, how can I help to make sure our time is used more wisely in session 6?
- Are there any members who may need extra encouragement this week? Note whether a card or phone call would be appropriate; then remember to follow up on each one.
- What was my overall impression of session 5?

3. Read through "Before the Session" on page 12 so that you will know what preparations you'll need to make before your next session.

JUST BETWEEN US

You made it! You're halfway through the journey and, though your sandals are looking worn, you are being transformed into His likeness with ever-increasing glory, which comes from the Lord, who is the Spirit (2 Cor. 3:18). God blesses nothing more than He rewards the pursuit of His Son. Not only are you in hot pursuit, you are leading others to do the same. Beloved, the rewards are guaranteed. If you're like me, however, you're finding that Christ is His own reward. Oh, how I would love to pour you a cup of tea and encourage you face-to-face. I feel such a sweet tie to my facilitators. I wish I could demonstrate how much I appreciate you. I will simply ask God to do something out of the ordinary for you this week. Be watching for it!

Notes

_____

_____

_____

_____

_____

_____

_____

_____

_____

_____

_____

_____

_____

_____

SESSION 6
The Necessity

BEFORE THE SESSION
Refer to page 12 for a description of session procedures.

Child Care Open, Attendance and Homework Check (15 min.)

DURING THE SESSION
Large Group—Welcome, Worship, and Prayer (15 min.)
1. Greet each member as she arrives and give her the name tag she used in the introductory session. Learn to call every participant by name.
2. Lead a time of worship and praise.
3. Pray, asking for God's presence and blessing throughout the session.
4. Dismiss to small groups.

Small Groups (45 min.)
1. Ask for prayer requests and have prayer (5 min.).
2. Review the week's Principal Questions and Personal Discussion Questions (40 min.).

Day 1:
- *Principal Question:* To what part of the father's request did Christ take exception in Mark 9:23?
- *Personal Discussion:* When was the last time your confidence was shaken and you were unable to do what God had empowered you to do?

Day 2:
- *Principal Question:* What two events had taken place in Luke 9:28-43 that may have provided a breeding ground for the greatness question in Luke 9:46?
- *Personal Discussion:* How might these two simultaneous events have provided a breeding ground for comparisons and discussions of greatness?

Day 3:
- *Principal Question:* What did Christ establish as the primary cause for joy for the seventy-two?
- *Personal Discussion:* Why would we be very wise to find our joy in who we are because of Him, rather than what we can do because of Him?

Day 4:
- *Principal Question:* Based on the account in Luke 10:25-37, and using one sentence, how would you define *neighbor*?
- *Personal Discussion:* When in your experience has the least expected person come to the rescue?

Day 5:
- *Principal Question:* Which one did Jesus love: Mary or Martha? What does that tell you?
- *Personal Discussion:* What tends to distract you from listening to God?

If time allows, ask in what ways God spoke directly to members in week 6.

Conclude 40-minute discussion time by affirming your members in their participation today and their grasp of the material. If you are using the optional video, move into large group to view the video or turn on the video in the one small group. If you are not viewing the video lecture, you may dismiss with a few introductory words about week 7 and a closing prayer.

Break and Return to Large Group (5 min.)

View the Video Presentation (50 min.)

Conclude Session (5 min.)
- Leader gives a brief response to the video in one or two sentences.
- Leader gives a brief introduction to week 7 in her own words and encourages them toward the completion of their home study.
- Leader closes with prayer. Again, since prayer requests were taken at the beginning of discussion, they are unnecessary at this time.
- Leader takes up name tags as group departs.

AFTER THE SESSION
1. Immediately record any concerns or impressions you had to pray for any member of your group while it is still fresh on your mind. Remember to pray for these throughout the week.
2. Evaluate session 6 by asking yourself the following questions and recording your answers:

- Was I adequately prepared for today's session?
- Was I able to begin and end session 6 on time?
- If not, how can I help to make sure our time is used more wisely in session 7?
- Do any members need extra encouragement this week? Note whether a card or phone call would be appropriate; then remember to follow up on each one.
- What was my overall impression of session 6?

3. Read through "Before the Session" on page 12 so that you will know what preparations you'll need to make before your next session.

JUST BETWEEN US

How are things going in your life about now? Are you captivated by the love of Christ, finding yourself increasingly drawn into His life story? Or is Satan having a fit at your expense? Maybe an odd concoction of the two?

Listen, Dear Leader. The enemy has no authority over you. If he's beginning to demonstrate just how unhappy he is that you are leading others to Christ, tell him who's Boss. And, by the way, that's not you or me. That's God. God's Word says that when we're doing His will, we can expect opposition. Don't let it get to you. Get back at the opposition with the Sword of the Spirit, the Word of God. Let's be careful to practice what we preach, Dear Leader, and fight the good fight of faith. You are more than an overcomer, and I'm so thankful to be on your team.

Notes

_____

_____

_____

_____

_____

_____

_____

_____

_____

_____

_____

_____

_____

_____

SESSION 7
The Infinite Treasure

BEFORE THE SESSION
Refer to page 12 for a description of session procedures.

Child Care Open, Attendance and Homework Check (15 min.)

DURING THE SESSION
Large Group—Welcome, Worship, and Prayer (15 min.)
1. Greet each member as she arrives and give her the name tag she used in the introductory session. Learn to call every participant by name.
2. Lead a time of worship and praise.
3. Pray, asking for God's presence and blessing throughout the session.
4. Dismiss to small groups.

Small Groups (45 min.)
1. Ask for prayer requests and have prayer (5 min.).
2. Review the week's Principal Questions and Personal Discussion Questions (40 min.).

Day 1:
- *Principal Question:* What do you think is represented by "a strong man" and "someone stronger"?
- *Personal Discussion:* Can you think of ways God has already divided with you some of the spoils of Satan's defeat?

Day 2:
- *Principal Question:* Of what did Jesus say we do not need to be afraid?
- *Personal Discussion:* In what ways can we guard against greed?

Day 3:
- *Principal Question:* What are the descriptions of a *faithful servant* implied in Luke 12:35-48?
- *Personal Discussion:* Give a few examples of what you think might constitute spiritual abuse.

Day 4:
- *Principal Question:* What dimension of Christ is illuminated in Luke 13:34?

- *Personal Discussion:* Personalize Psalm 17:7-9 as if every word were written just to you. How do the verses express your own words of faith and gratitude to God?

Day 5:
- *Principal Question:* In Luke 15 what common theme do all three parables share?
- *Personal Discussion:* What kinds of things motivate a person to leave a healthy, loving, and even wealthy environment?

If time allows, ask ways in which God spoke directly to members in week 7.

Conclude 40-minute discussion time by affirming your members in their participation today and their apparent grasp of the material. If you are using the optional video, move into large group to view the video or turn on the video in the one small group. If you are not viewing the video, you may dismiss with a few introductory words about week 8 and a closing prayer.

Break and Return to Large Group (5 min.)

View the Video Presentation (50 min.)

Conclude Session (5 min.)
- Leader gives a brief response to the video in one or two sentences.
- Leader gives a brief introduction to week 8 in her own words and encourages them toward the completion of their home study.
- Leader closes with prayer. Again, since prayer requests were taken at the beginning of discussion, they would not be necessary at this time.
- Leader takes up name tags as group departs.

AFTER THE SESSION
1. Immediately record any concerns or impressions you had to pray for any member of your group while it is still fresh on your mind. Remember to pray for these throughout the week.
2. Evaluate session 7 by asking yourself the following questions and recording your answers:

- Was I adequately prepared for today's session?
- Was I able to begin and end session 7 on time?
- If not, how can I help make sure our time is used more wisely in session 8?
- Do any members need extra encouragement this week? Note whether a card or phone call would be appropriate; then remember to follow up.
- What was my overall impression of session 7?

3. Read through "Before the Session" on page 12 so that you will know what preparations you'll need to make before your next session.

JUST BETWEEN US

Dear Leader, I wonder week-to-week what God is whispering to your soul and how He's applying these truths to your precious life. I urge you to keep a journal—a record of God's faithfulness. Your journey with Him is completely personal and unique. No one shares exactly the same one. I want you to savor every minute of it. God can use exactly the same Scripture to speak to a dozen different people in a dozen different ways. In the midst of your busy schedule, don't forget to listen to Him whisper. The most personal things God has to say to you will often be spoken in a still, small voice.

Take your time with Him. Let Him speak to you and love you uniquely.

Notes

_____

_____

_____

_____

_____

_____

_____

_____

_____

_____

_____

_____

_____

SESSION 8
The Answer

BEFORE THE SESSION
Refer to page 12 for a description of session procedures.

Child Care Open, Attendance and Homework Check (15 min.)

DURING THE SESSION
Large Group—Welcome, Worship, and Prayer (15 min.)
1. Greet each member as she arrives and give her the name tag she used in the introductory session. Learn to call every participant by name.
2. Lead a time of worship and praise.
3. Pray, asking for God's presence and blessing throughout the session.
4. Dismiss to small groups.

Small Groups (45 min.)
1. Ask for prayer requests and have prayer (5 min.).
2. Review the week's Principal Questions and Personal Discussion Questions (40 min.).

Day 1:
• *Principal Question:* How did Christ picture the seriousness of causing another person to sin?
• *Personal Discussion:* Difficult-to-forgive circumstances can set a trap. How does Satan use unforgiveness as bait to entrap us in sin (2 Cor. 2:10-11)?

Day 2:
• *Principal Question:* What evidence do you see of "spot counting" in Luke 18:9-14?
• *Personal Discussion:* Can you describe an experience with a group of people that eclipsed all the differences and reminded you how much you were all the same?

Day 3:
• *Principal Question:* What critical difference between separates believing Christ to be good and believing Christ to be God?

• *Personal Discussion:* How did you fare throughout our game? Check just one answer.
  ❑ Just call me perfection personified.
  ❑ My halo may be slipping a bit.
  ❑ I was thrown out of the game in the first inning, quarter, or whatever.

Day 4:
• *Principal Question:* What insight about Zacchaeus' wealth do you see in Proverbs 15:27 and 28:25?
• *Personal Discussion:* What is the most marked difference you see that Christ has made in your life, whether in demeanor or life-practice?

Day 5:
• *Principal Question:* According to Luke 12:40, why would forecasting a time of Christ's return be a waste of time?
• *Personal Discussion:* When did you last deeply yearn for Christ to return and to right all wrongs?

If time allows, ask ways in which God spoke directly to members in week 8.

Conclude 40-minute discussion time by affirming your members in their participation today and their apparent grasp of the material. If you are using the optional video, move into large group to view the video or turn on the video in the one small group. If you are not viewing the video, you may dismiss with a few introductory words about week 9 and a closing prayer.

Break and Return to Large Group (5 min.)

View the Video Presentation (50 min.)

Conclude Session (5 min.)
• Leader gives a brief response to the video in one or two sentences.
• Leader gives a brief introduction to week 9 in her own words and encourages them toward the completion of their home study.

- Leader closes with prayer. Again, since prayer requests were taken at the beginning of discussion, they would not be necessary at this time.
- Leader takes up name tags as group departs.

AFTER THE SESSION

1. Immediately record any concerns or impressions you had to pray for any member of your group while it is still fresh on your mind. Remember to pray for these throughout the week.
2. Evaluate session 8 by asking yourself the following questions and recording your answers:

- Was I adequately prepared for today's session?
- Was I able to begin and end session 8 on time?
- If not, how can I help make sure our time is used more wisely in session 9?
- Are there any members who may need extra encouragement this week? Note whether a card or phone call would be appropriate; then remember to follow up on each one.
- What was my overall impression of session 8?

3. Read through "Before the Session" on page 12 so that you will know what preparations you'll need to make before your next session.

JUST BETWEEN US

I am praying so hard that you are already inheriting a blessing from your willingness to serve God as a facilitator of this Bible study. You are actively encouraging others to know and love Jesus Christ, the Savior of the world. What could God possibly esteem more? As you encourage others, make sure that you stay encouraged. Are you by any chance about to "run out of steam"? In the life of the believer, that figure of speech represents a vivid spiritual reality. When our "out-pour" exceeds our "in-take," we run out of the steam of the Holy Spirit. No, He will never leave us, but we can certainly experience the depletion of His filling. Without the empowering of the Holy Spirit, we're trying to drive a car with no gas by our own determination. Not only is it fruitless, it's no fun! I want you to have some fun with God! Here's your assignment this week: do something fun with God—something out of the ordinary like going to the park and taking a walk with Him, attending a Christian concert, or taking part in something entirely different at another church … maybe even another denomination, for heaven's sake! Go ahead—live a little!

Notes

_____

_____

_____

_____

_____

_____

_____

_____

_____

SESSION 9

The Lamb of God

BEFORE THE SESSION

Refer to page 12 for a description of session procedures.

Child Care Open, Attendance and Homework Check (15 min.)

DURING THE SESSION

Large Group—Welcome, Worship, and Prayer (15 min.)

1. Greet each member as she arrives and give her the name tag she used in the introductory session. Learn to call every participant by name.
2. Lead a time of worship and praise.
3. Pray, asking for God's presence and blessing throughout the session.
4. Dismiss to small groups.

Small Groups (45 min.)

1. Ask for prayer requests and have prayer (5 min.).
2. Review the week's Principal Questions and Personal Discussion Questions (40 min.).

Day 1:

- *Principal Question:* How did Judas and the chief priests/teachers of the law become the means to an end to one another?
- *Personal Discussion:* How does Christ's response in Matthew 16:23 illustrate that Satan capitalizes on man's own self-centered interests?

Day 2:

- *Principal Question:* What was Jesus' attitude toward observing the Passover with His disciples?
- *Personal Discussion:* Read back over the words of the Kiddush (p. 198). Which part of it seems especially meaningful as you imagine the words coming from the mouth of Christ? Why?

Day 3:

- *Principal Question:* What do you think Christ meant when He used this figure of speech to Peter: "Satan has asked to sift you as wheat" (Luke 22:31)?

- *Personal Discussion:* List every hint you see that Peter used what he learned to strengthen fellow brothers and sisters like you and me, helping us to stand.

Day 4:

- *Principal Question:* According to Matthew 26:53, what could Christ have done rather than allow Himself to be arrested?
- *Personal Discussion:* What is your reaction when you consider that God could have spared Jesus' suffering and chosen to let us bear the consequences of our own sin?

Day 5:

- *Principal Question:* Based on your memory of our present journey through Luke, can you identify a few of Peter's encounters with Christ that make his denial more startling?
- *Personal Discussion:* Are you relating with Peter on any level at this point? ❏ Yes ❏ No If so, how?

If time allows, ask ways in which God spoke directly to members in week 9.

Conclude 40-minute discussion time by affirming your members in their participation today and their apparent grasp of the material. If you are using the optional video, move into large group to view the video or turn on the video in the one small group. If you are not viewing the video, you may dismiss with a few introductory words about week 10 and a closing prayer.

Break and Return to Large Group (5 min.)

View the Video Presentation (50 min.)

Conclude Session (5 min.)

- Leader gives a brief response to the video in one or two sentences.
- Leader gives a brief introduction to week 8 in her own words and encourages them toward the completion of their home study.
- Leader closes with prayer.
- Leader takes up name tags as group departs.

28

AFTER THE SESSION

1. Immediately record any concerns or impressions you had to pray for any member of your group while it is still fresh on your mind. Remember to pray for these throughout the week.
2. Evaluate session 9 by asking yourself the following questions and recording your answers:
   - Was I adequately prepared for today's session?
   - Do any members need extra encouragement this week? Note whether a card or phone call would be appropriate; then remember to follow up.
   - What was my overall impression of session 9?
3. Read through "Before the Session" on page 12 as a reminder of the preparations you'll need to make before your final session.

JUST BETWEEN US

Dear Leader, have you surrendered your precious life to the cross of Christ? To be crucified with Him? You've given God so much, Beloved. But now He wants the rest—not to hurt you or cheat you, but to bless you beyond your wildest imagination. Our enemy and our flesh try to convince us that the crucified life is a mammoth sacrifice but, when all is said and done, the far greater sacrifice will be to have missed the fullness of life God had for us.

God is not calling you to figuratively hang on that cross as the living dead for the rest of your life. Remember, He is calling you to be crucified with Christ. Jesus certainly didn't stay on the cross. He rose from the dead! God wants to raise you to resurrection life, Dear One, so that He can live through you. The crucified life is not the life of the martyr. Rather, it's the life of one who can say, "God did more than my eyes had ever seen, ears had ever heard, and my mind had ever conceived!" (1 Cor. 2:9). That's what He has prepared for you!

Notes

_____

_____

_____

_____

_____

_____

_____

_____

_____

SESSION 10

The Risen Hope

BEFORE THE SESSION
Refer to page 12 for a description of session procedures.

Child Care Open, Attendance and Homework Check (15 min.)

DURING THE SESSION
Large Group—Welcome, Worship, and Prayer (15 min.)
1. Greet each member as she arrives.
2. Lead a time of worship and praise.
3. Pray, asking for God's presence and blessing throughout the session.
4. Dismiss to small groups.

Small Groups (45 min.)
1. Ask for prayer requests and have prayer (5 min.).
2. Review the week's Principal Questions and Personal Discussion Questions (40 min.).

Day 1:
- *Principal Question:* Why was Pilate necessary?
- *Personal Discussion:* In the margin list a few things about Christ you think might have surged such vehement envy in the religious leaders.

Day 2:
- *Principal Question:* According to Colossians 2:13-14, what was nailed to His cross?
- *Personal Discussion:* What kinds of things might Simon have been thinking or feeling as he carried Jesus' cross?

Day 3:
- *Principal Question:* What did Mary Magdalene and the other Mary find at the tomb?
- *Personal Discussion:* What do you think each of the following was thinking about the other at that meeting: Joseph about Pilate? Pilate about Joseph?

Day 4:
- *Principal Question:* What was the mood of Cleopas and his companion when Christ asked what they were discussing?

- *Personal Discussion:* Can you think of a time when Christ walked beside you but you did not recognize Him until "after the fact"? If so, share briefly.

Day 5:
- *Principal Question:* What special significance do Christ's words in Luke 24:36 have as conveyed in Ephesians 2:14?
- *Personal Question:* Christ did not have to retain the scars in His resurrected body. Why do you think He did?

If time allows, ask what ways God spoke directly to members in week 10.

Conclude the 40-minute discussion time by affirming their participation throughout the last 10 weeks and their grasp of material that was often difficult. If you are using the optional video, move into large group to view the last segment or turn on the video in the one small group. If you are not using the video, you may dismiss with concluding remarks and a closing prayer at this time.

Break and Return to Large Group (5 min.)

View the Video Presentation (50 min.)

Conclude Session (10 min. rather than 5, if you are doing an optional evaluation)
- If you prepared an evaluation, distribute it at this time and allow 5 minutes to complete it.
- Leader offers closing remarks to *Jesus the One and Only.*
- Leader closes with prayer.
- Leader has a good laugh or a good cry depending on which seems appropriate!

AFTER THE SESSION
1. Evaluate session 10 by asking yourself the following concluding questions and recording your answers:
   - Did members seem to grasp the overall principles emphasized in this 10-week study?
   - Are there group members with no church home who I should invite to visit church with me?
   - Should I remain in contact with any members of

my group for the purpose of encouragement?
- Would I consider taking another course of this kind?
- Would I consider leading another course of this kind?
- What was my overall impression of *Jesus the One and Only?*

2. Consider letting us hear from you. If God has spoken to you or done something significant in your life or the lives of one of your members as a direct result of this Bible study, we would love for you to share a brief testimony with us. Write to us, including your name, address, phone number, and church affiliation, and mail your testimony to:

Leadership and Adult Publishing
Dale McCleskey, Editor-in-Chief
One LifeWay Plaza
Nashville, Tennessee 37234-0175

JUST BETWEEN US

I wish I had the words to express my gratitude to you. I am so honored to have partnered with you in this journey. I hold you in very high esteem and regard you as better than myself. If I could, I would wash your feet, Faithful Servant. You have worked hard and now this specific task is complete. In a way, isn't that the greatest feeling? You finished! God's work through this 10-week journey, however, is far from being finished. You can find great joy in knowing that He will continue His good work in every member of your group. And not only in them, but also in you. Every bit of energy expended for the sake of Christ will bear eternal fruit. You put in 10 weeks. God puts in an eternity. Not a bad deal, is it? Take a little while to rest in Him. To reflect on the journey. To journal perhaps. Soak it all in by meditating on Him and all He's shown you. Don't move so quickly to the next assignment that you miss the postscript. After every harvest, there never fails to be fruit left behind in the field. Go back and glean, Dear One. All by yourself. The leftovers are all yours. Thank you, Beloved. I love you.

Notes

_____

_____

_____

_____

_____

_____

_____

_____

_____

SESSIONS 1-10
Video Response Sheet Answers

Introductory Session

not to prophesy; hard as flint, would not listen; stopped talking; 1. Alexander; 2. seventy; 3. Jewish law; 4. "King of the Jews"; hearing the words of the Lord; 1. identity; set them apart; 2. a hunger; to make full; full; empty; go; came; famine, fullness; withholding; revealing

Session 1

Event 1: Mary, Nazareth; Event 2: hill country, Judea; skip, leap, dance, joy; Event 3: dream, Joseph; with us; Event 4: took, home; Event 5: traveled, Bethlehem; Event 6: Jesus Christ, born; Event 7: shepherds; Event 8: baby, Bethlehem; Event 9: circumcised Event 10: presented to the Lord; Event 11: visit, Magi; Event 12: escaped, Egypt; Event 13: raised, manhood

Session 2

1. preparation; beaten pathway; 2. location; Jesus, Joshua; consecrate, qadhash; pala, wonders; 3. visitation; 4. representation; 5. demonstration; 6. proclamation

Session 3

future, suffers; fullness; unfair, unfair; 1. kingdom, heaven; 2. satisfied; hungry, famished, starved; 3. laugh; 4. hated, excluded, rejected; separate, cast out; enemies; must, sincere; good; curse; Pray; called

Session 4

1. called, He, going; 2. tossed; inexperienced; 3. danger 4. destroyed; 5. dominion, all things; 1. "Where is your faith?"' 2. "Who is this?"

Session 5

1. readjust, vision; willing, receive, willing, reveal; fullness, security, mystery; emotional, mental; 2. rearrange, surroundings; 3. immortal, revelation; 4. build, stay; beneficial; harmonious; 5. private, through us; 6. hearing, sight; 7. alone; 8. mountaintop, transfigured

Session 6

relationships; change; know, understand; think, still higher; return, baffled; teach, how, pray; 1. place; environment; practice; 2. position; Father, child; 3. perspective; King; heaven, hallowed; 4. priority; His will, accomplished; 5. petition; day-by-day; 6. pardon; forgiveness, incentive; 7. preparation; directly approaching, in advance; 8. persistence; keep praying

Session 7

weakness, righteousness; praise; heart, man; triumphs; recognizable; peace; every external expression, grief; what, need; vulnerable, attack; Father's house; hot, fervent; jealous; passion

Session 8

1. Difficult, stone's throw; 2. Deliberate, as usual; nothing; where. going; 3. Disciple's, learn; learner, pupil; teacher; know, own; 4. Determined, knelt down; war, will; crisis, God-man; consumed, will, other; draws back, continues on; cup; 5. Depth, forward, back; 6. Divine, Jesus Christ

Session 9

1. dark land; full bloom, ripeness, vigor; both; spirits; permission, power; 2. torn veil; top, bottom; 3. loud voice; Word; voice, volume; 4. last breath; 5. borrowed tomb; 6. distant crowd

Session 10

1. great joy; 2. Jesus Christ; 3. instructions; 4. convincing; 5. power; 6. witnesses Samarias; facts, tidings; death; 7. imminent, literal